My First
Nature Treasury

from the Editors of *Chickadee* Magazine

Written by Lizann Flatt

Illustrated by

Allan Cormack and Deborah Drew-Brook

Sierra Club Books for Children

San Francisco

The Sierra Club, founded in 1892 by John Muir, has devoted itself to the study and protection of the earth's scenic and ecological resources—mountains, wetlands, woodlands, wild shores and rivers, deserts and plains. The publishing program of the Sierra Club offers books to the public as a nonprofit educational service in the hope that they may enlarge the public's understanding of the Club's basic concerns. The point of view expressed in each book, however, does not necessarily represent that of the Club. The Sierra Club has some sixty chapters in the United States and in Canada. For information about how you may participate in its programs to preserve wilderness and the quality of life, please address inquiries to Sierra Club, 730 Polk Street, San Francisco, CA 94109.

First U.S. Edition 1995

First Published in Canada by Greey de Pencier Books

Library of Congress Cataloging-in-Publication Data

Flatt, Lizann.
My first nature treasury / from the editors of Chickadee magazine;
by Lizann Flatt; illustrated by Allan Cormack and Deborah Drew-Brook.
p. cm.
ISBN 0-87156-362-2
1. Nature—Juvenile literature. 2. Natural history—Juvenile literature. [1. Nature. 2. Natural history.] I. Drew-Brook-Cormack, Allan, ill. II. Drew-Brook-Cormack, Deborah, ill. III. Chickadee. IV. Title. V. Title: Nature treasury.
QH48.F587 1995
508—dc20 94-38046

Printed in Hong Kong

10 9 8 7 6 5 4 3 2 1

Contents

Exploring Nature

From the tiniest flower to the largest whale, every living thing on our planet is a part of nature. Exploring nature means discovering a new mix of living things everywhere you look.

Have you ever been to a desert? How about to the Arctic or to the bottom of the ocean? Well, we are going to take you there so that you can see the amazing plants and animals that live in these places. You'll climb in tree habitats: a forest and a rain forest. You'll roam the grasslands: prairie, savanna and tundra. You'll wander across a harsh and hot desert. Then you'll dive down into the water to explore a lake, a river, an ocean and a coral reef.

Along the way, you'll find out some incredible secrets of nature. Did you know that just a few things on Earth make it possible for all plants and animals to live? You'll get a really close-up look at water, air, trees, soil and grass. You'll discover many different families of animals and plants, what they eat, and how they grow.

And there's something special for you to do, too.

cheetah

Whenever you see animals or plants on a black circle, like these,

ground squirrel

bison

butterfly

find as many of them as you can in the picture. Look closely; they are all there somewhere.

Now, get ready for your exciting journey through nature around the world.

All Kinds of Animals

Animals are living things. They can use their senses (hearing, sight, smell, taste, touch) to take in what's around them, and they can move around whenever they choose.

Mammals feed their babies milk. Most mammals have fur or some kind of hair.

bat

lemur

zebra

whale

Birds have feathers and lay hard-shelled eggs.

kiwi

eagle

goose

Reptiles have dry, scaly skin, and they have to sit in the sun or shade to warm up or cool down.

turtle

snake

alligator

Amphibians are born in the water and have moist skin.

caecilian

frog

salamander

Fish have fins to help them move, and they live in water.

sawtooth shark

ray

seahorse

trout

Crustaceans have a hard skeleton on the outside and jointed legs.

wood louse

shrimp

water flea

Mollusks have soft bodies and use a foot or tentacles to move around. Some have a hard shell.

snail

nudibranch

octopus

Insects have six legs and a hard skeleton on the outside.

praying mantis

butterfly

ladybug

Arachnids have eight legs and a hard skeleton on the outside.

mite

scorpion

spider

How Animals Grow

Swallowtail Butterfly

4. The caterpillar sheds its outer covering again and forms a chrysalis. Inside the chrysalis changes are happening.

5. At last the chrysalis opens and out comes a butterfly.

Start here

1. Tiny mice are born. They're hungry for their mother's milk.

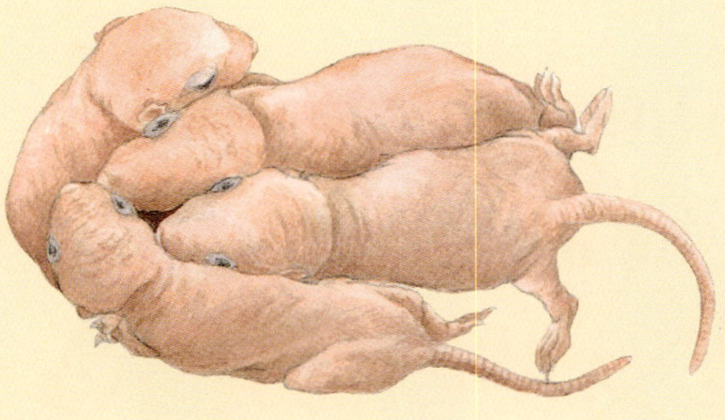

2. The mice grow more hair, but they still can't see or hear.

Start here

1. The female butterfly laid this egg. Then she flew away.

2. A little caterpillar hatches. It eats leaves to grow bigger.

3. The caterpillar crawls out of its hard outer covering many times as it grows.

Harvest Mouse

4. The grown-up mice can find food and take care of themselves.

3. Now the mice are furry. Their eyes and ears have opened.

Cardinal

4. Now the birds are grown. They can take care of themselves.

3. The chicks are fed so they will grow. Their feathers are growing, too.

Start here

1. The female crab has laid her eggs. She carries them around underneath her body.

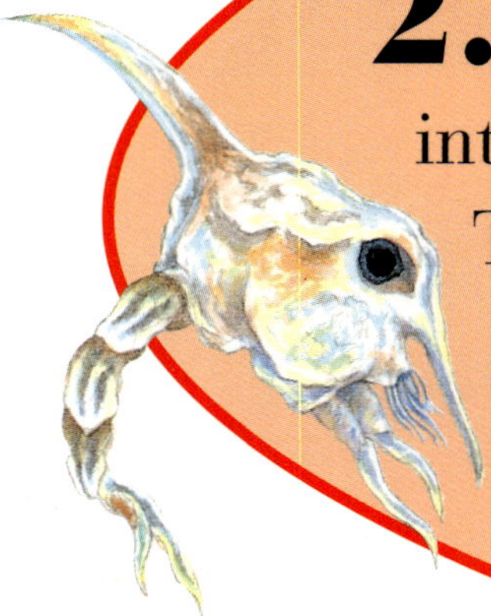

2. The eggs hatch into tiny larvae. They float in the sunny water and eat tiny plants.

3. Each larva crawls out of its hard outer covering many times as it grows. It looks different each time.

Start here

1. The female bird has laid her eggs. She sits on them to keep them warm.

2. The little chicks hatch from the eggs. They can't see for a few days.

Blue Crab

4. This baby sheds its outer covering again. Now it looks like an adult, but it's still small.

5. The crab keeps growing bigger and bigger by crawling out of its old outer covering.

Soil Up Close

What is soil made of?

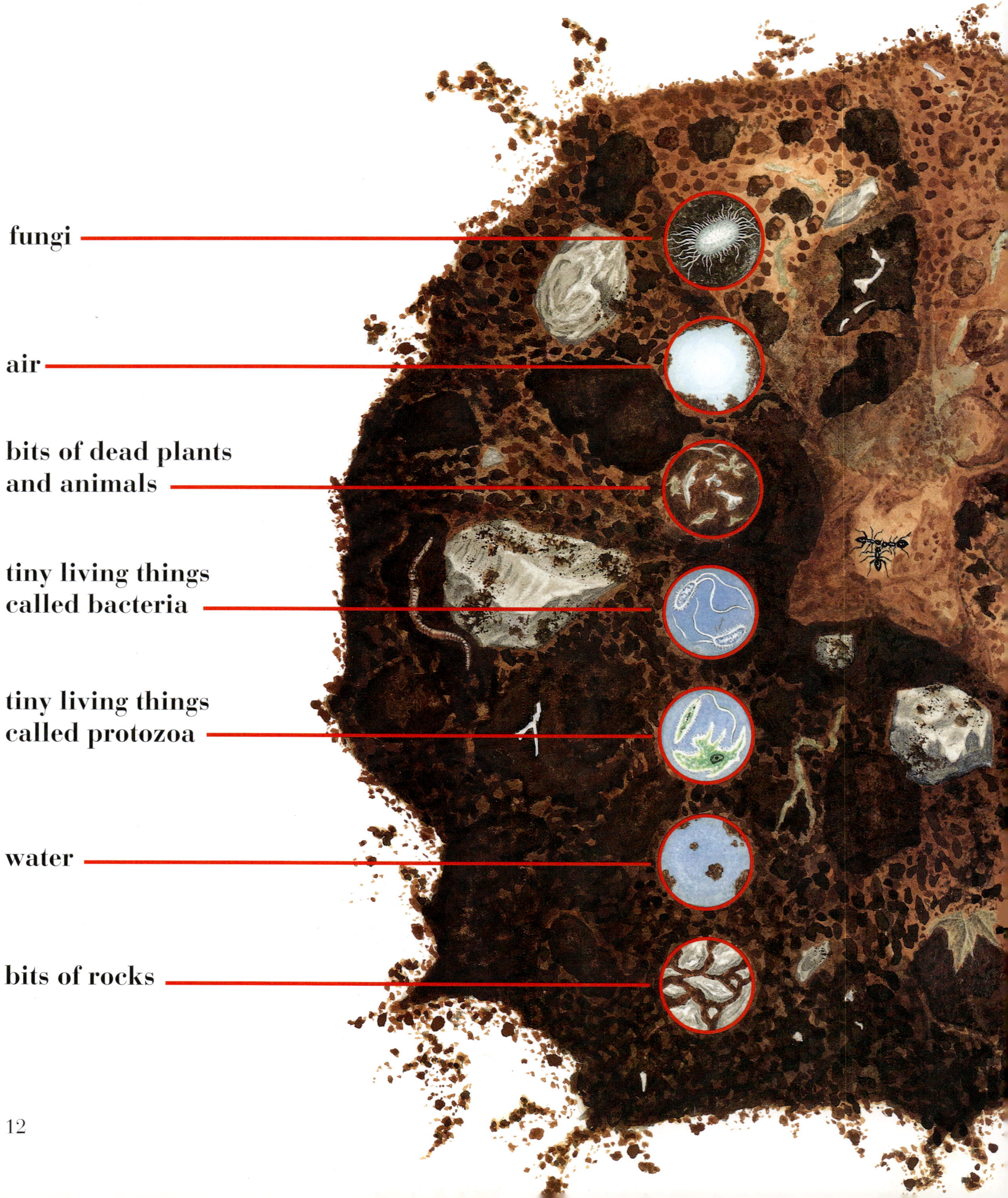

Soil helps plants grow, and plants are food for animals. Some animals even live in soil.

Soil is a thin layer on top of rock.

All Kinds of Plants

Plants are living things. They make their own food using sunshine, and they respond to changes in light, weather and other things around them.

Flowering plants have flowers that produce new seeds. These seeds are often inside a fruit.

pumpkin

buttercup

cherry tree

potato

Conifers and their relatives have seeds that are not inside a fruit. They often have cones that produce new seeds.

juniper

cycad

cedar

Bryophytes grow in damp, shady places. They are short and don't have any roots.

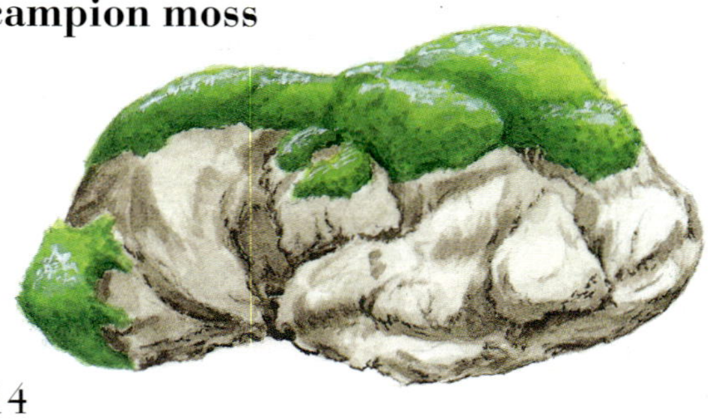
campion moss

liverwort

sphagnum moss

Ferns and their relatives grow in damp places. They have roots, but instead of seeds, they have spores.

march clubmoss

fern

horsetail

Algae live mostly in water. They don't have true roots. Instead, they absorb their food through their skin.

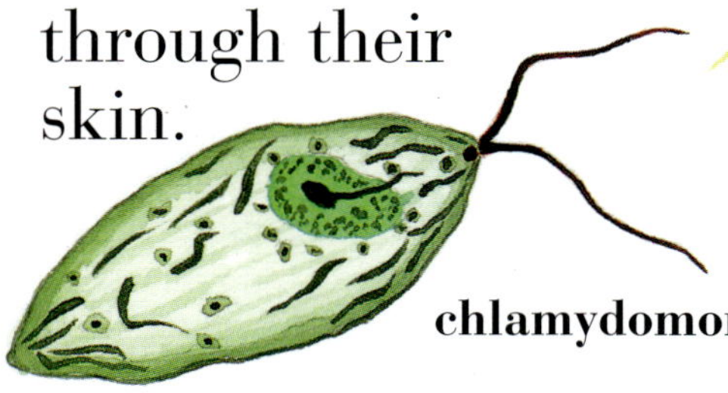

chlamydomonas

rockweed

sea lettuce

Fungi are not true plants, but they are closer to being plants than animals. They eat decaying material in the soil.

toadstool

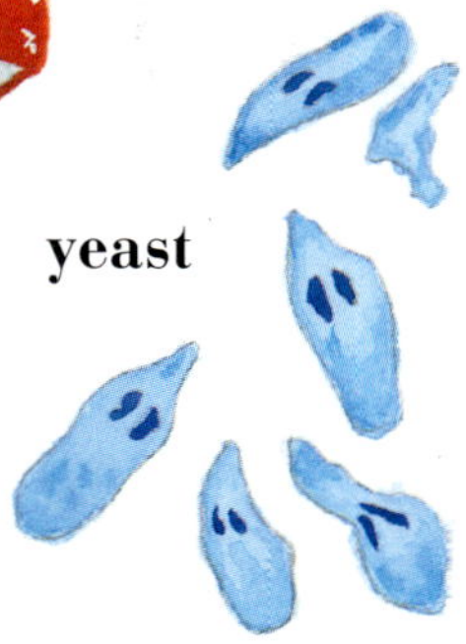

yeast

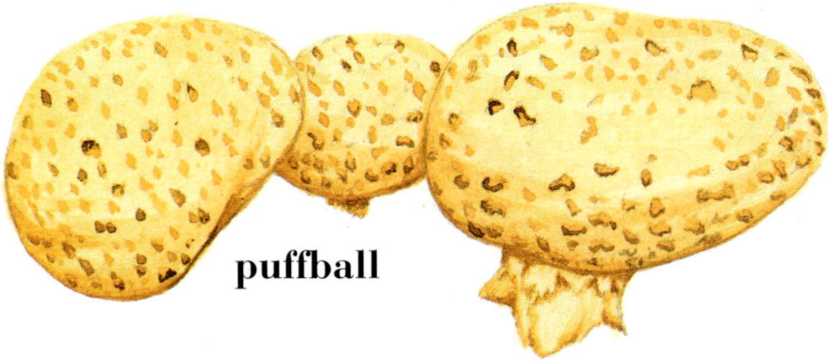

puffball

Lichens are part algae plant and part fungus. Intertwined, they help each other live.

beard lichen

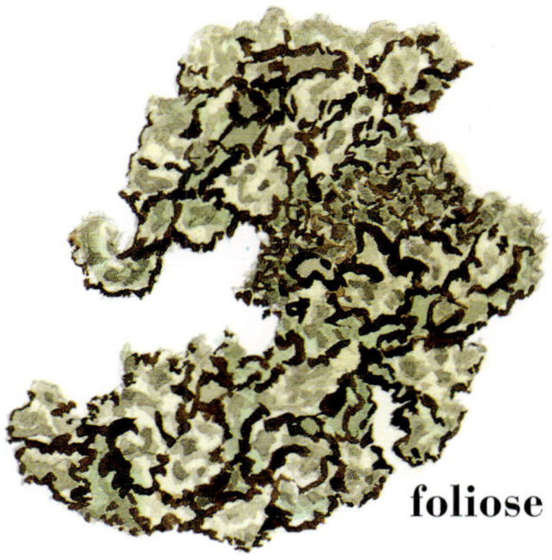

foliose lichen

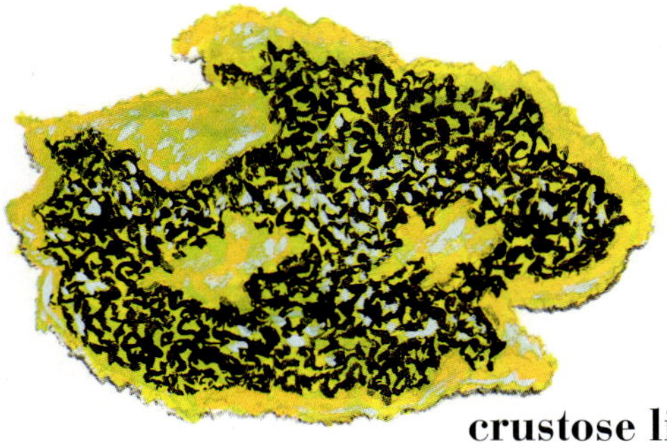

crustose lichen

How Plants Grow

Fern

4. The fern grows bigger as more fronds uncurl. Soon more spores will form on the underside of some fronds to grow new ferns.

3. A few roots and a tall frond begin to grow. The heart-shaped plant dies.

Start here

1. The milkweed fluff floats through the air. It lands on the ground and the seed falls off.

2. Soon a small sprout peeks out of the soil. The seed cover falls off.

3. The plant grows taller. More and more leaves appear, and the flowers open.

Start here

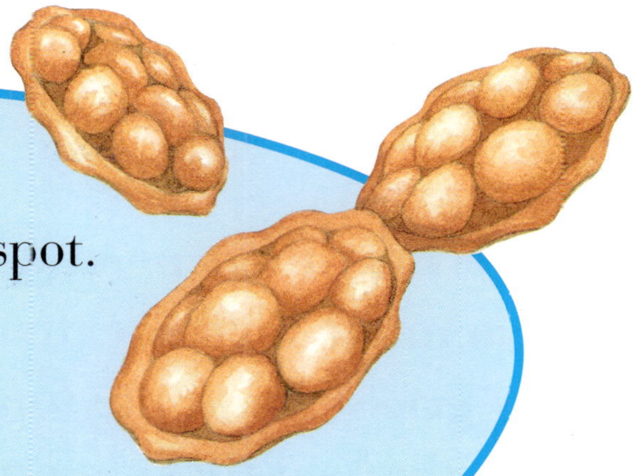

1. A tiny spore falls off a fern. It lands in a moist, shady spot.

2. The spore grows into a small, heart-shaped plant. Underneath this plant, egg cells develop into a tiny new plant.

4. Insects come to drink the sweet flower nectar, and pollen sticks to their feet. When the insects move on, the pollen sticks to other milkweed flowers.

5. The flowers with new pollen become pods. Soon the pods will split and milkweed fluff will blow away to grow new plants.

Milkweed

What Animals Eat

All living things need food. Plants on land and in water use sunlight to make food for themselves. Some animals eat plants such as grasses and phytoplankton. Other animals eat the animals that eat those plants. Sometimes bigger animals eat *them*.

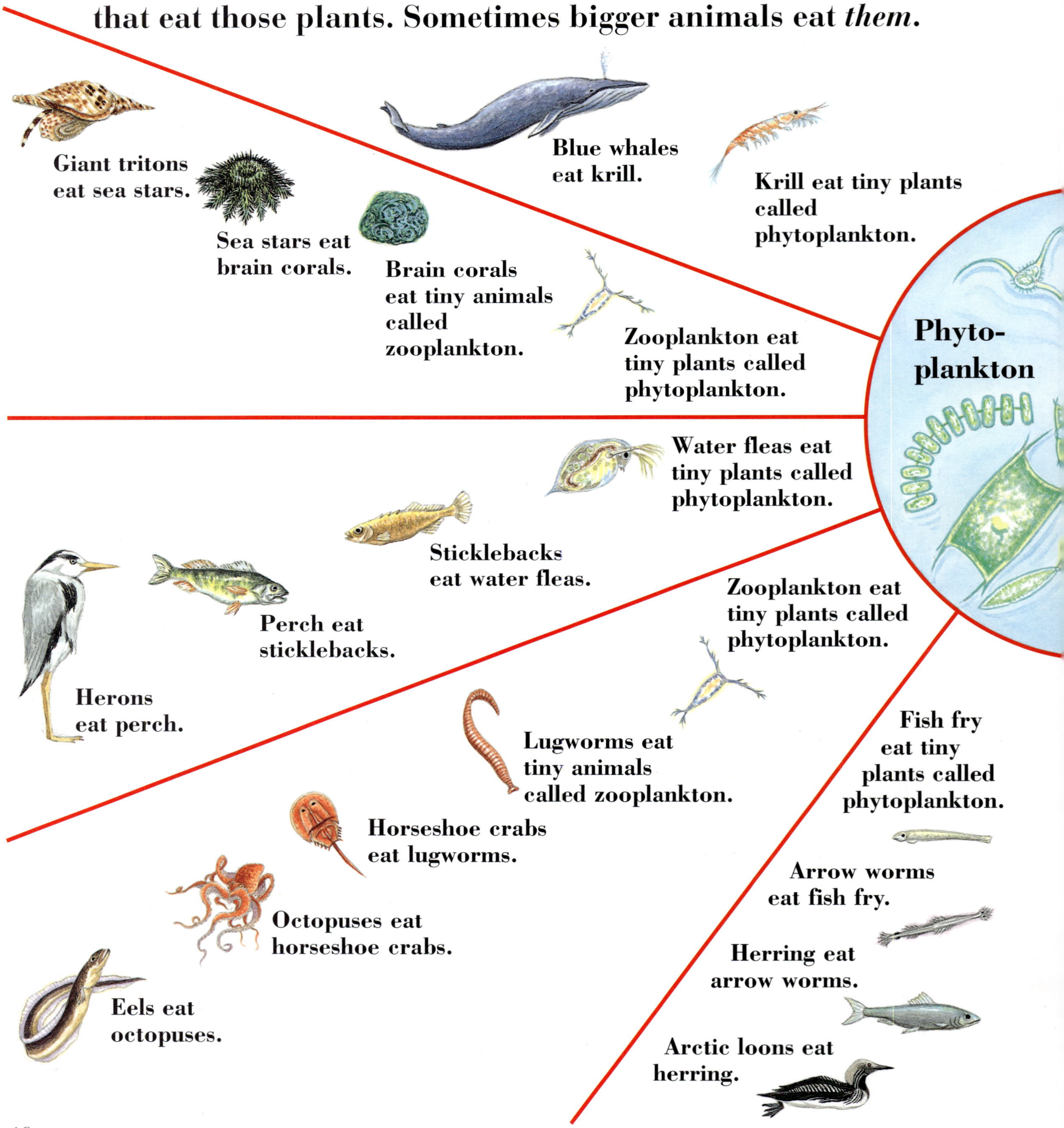

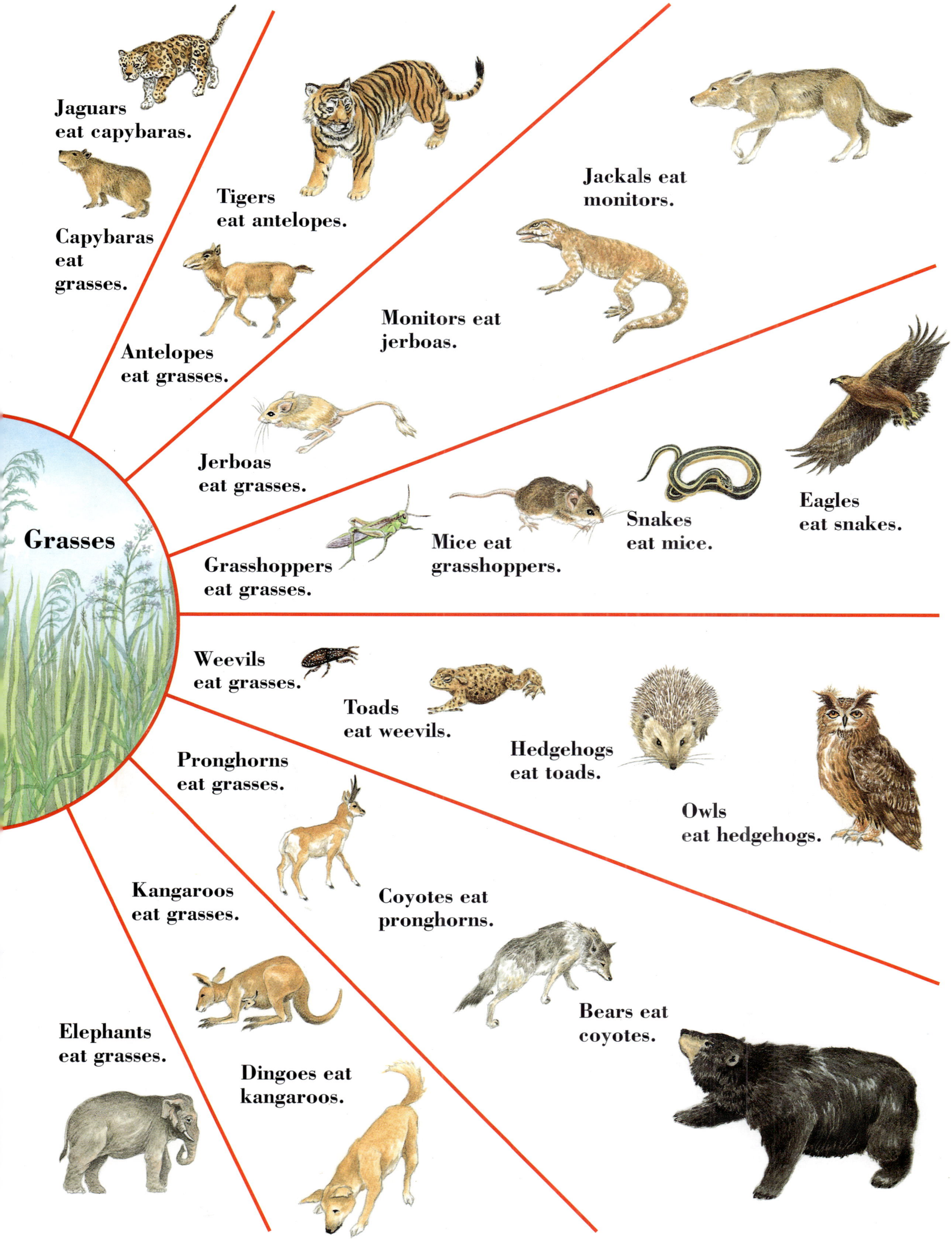
Grasses
Jaguars eat capybaras.
Capybaras eat grasses.
Tigers eat antelopes.
Antelopes eat grasses.
Jackals eat monitors.
Monitors eat jerboas.
Jerboas eat grasses.
Grasshoppers eat grasses.
Mice eat grasshoppers.
Snakes eat mice.
Eagles eat snakes.
Weevils eat grasses.
Toads eat weevils.
Hedgehogs eat toads.
Owls eat hedgehogs.
Pronghorns eat grasses.
Coyotes eat pronghorns.
Bears eat coyotes.
Kangaroos eat grasses.
Dingoes eat kangaroos.
Elephants eat grasses.

Trees Up Close

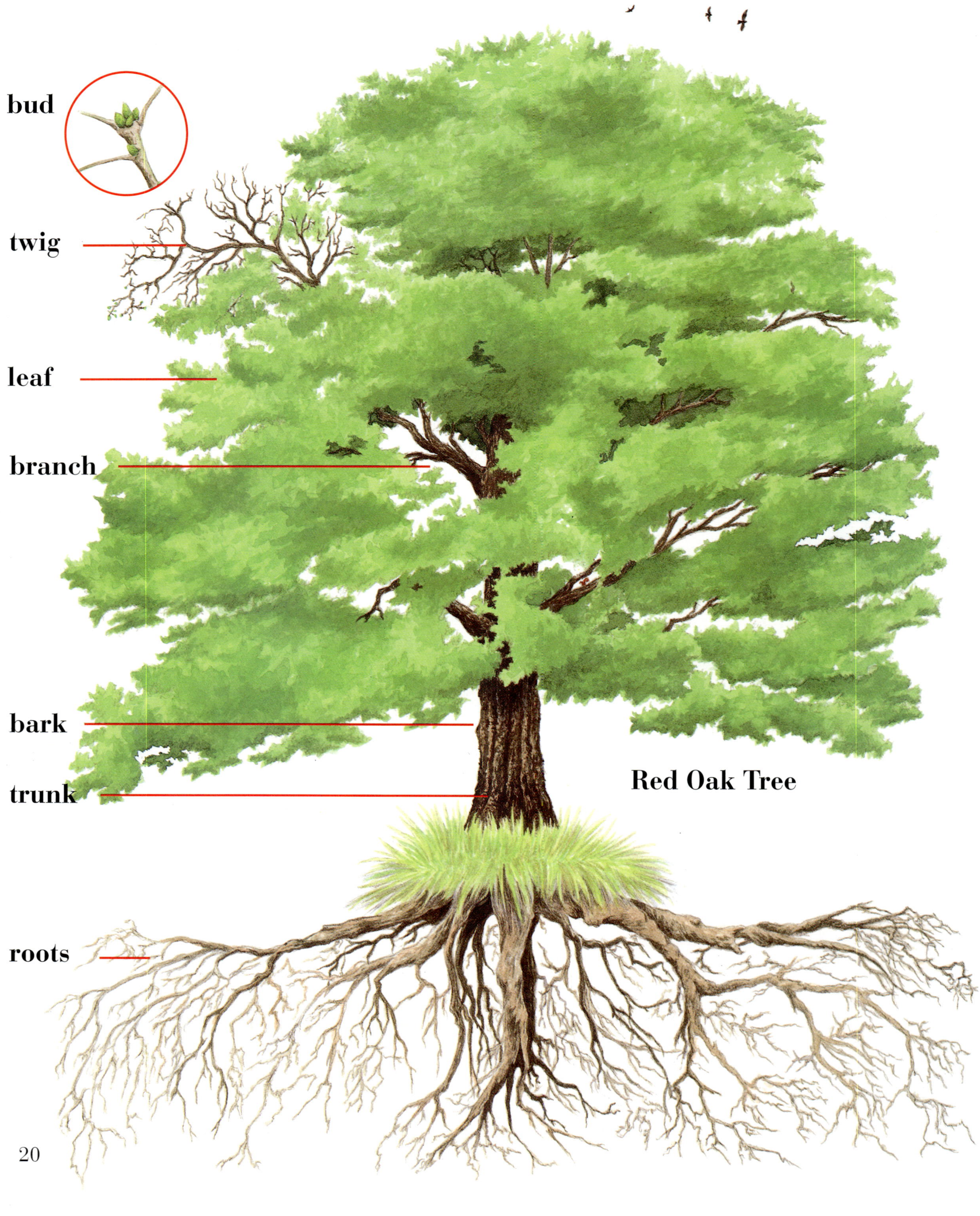

People, animals and plants need trees for food, shade and sometimes even for homes. Trees clean the air we breathe, too.

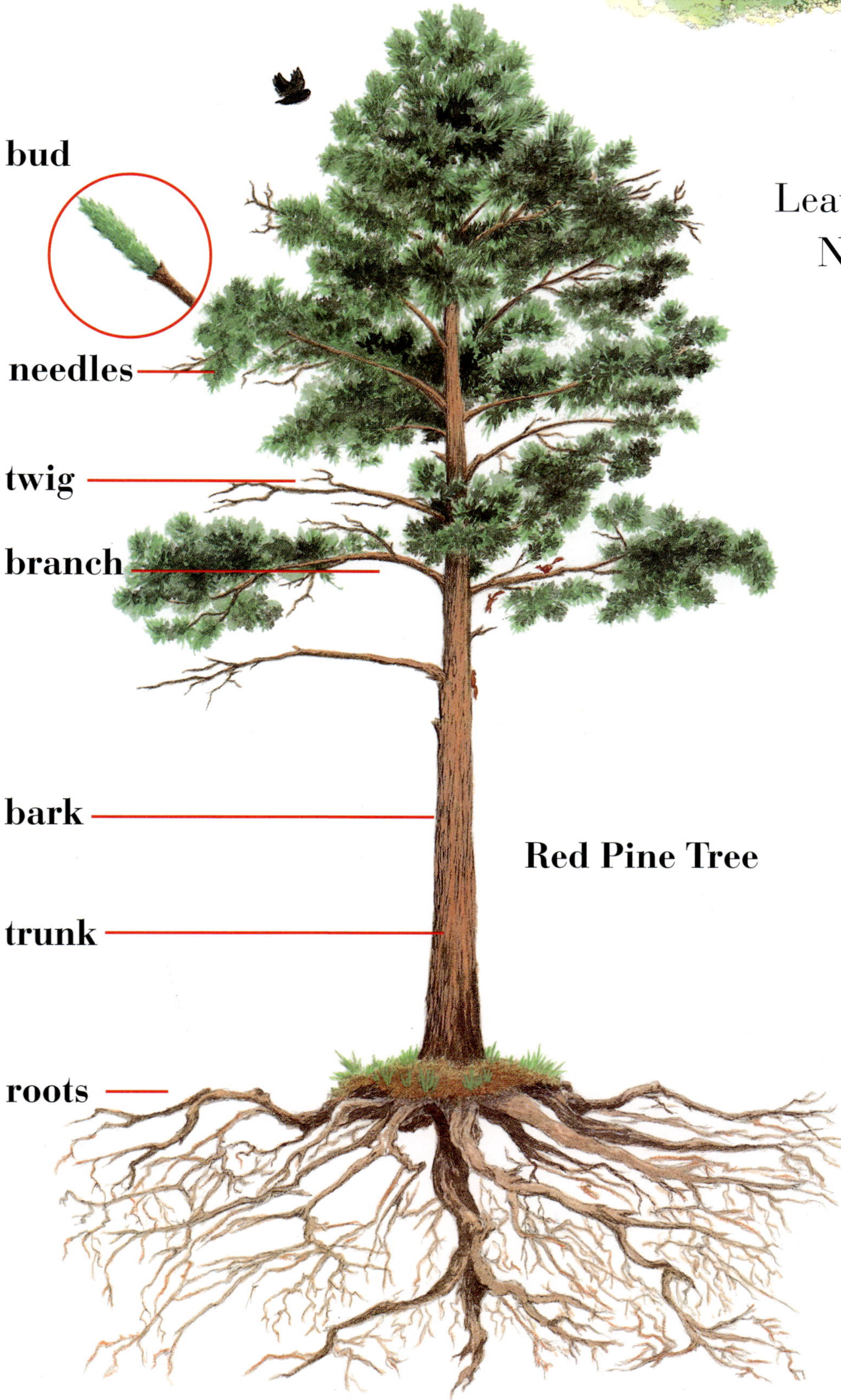

Red Pine Tree

Leaves can be many shapes. Needles are leaves, too.

red oak leaf

mountain ash leaf

white cedar needles

red pine needles

white birch leaf

Forest

goshawk
worm
carpenter ants
garter snake
red oak
rabbit
red pine
wood frog
chickadee

A North American mixed forest during the day.

RECYCLED LEAVES

Millipedes, springtails and worms eat fallen leaves. Their bodies digest the leaves and turn them into food for the soil.

Rain Forest

A South American rain forest during the day.

hummingbird
vine snake
marmoset
army ant
potoo
howler monkey
scarlet macaw
liana vine
sloth
harpy eagle

Grass Up Close

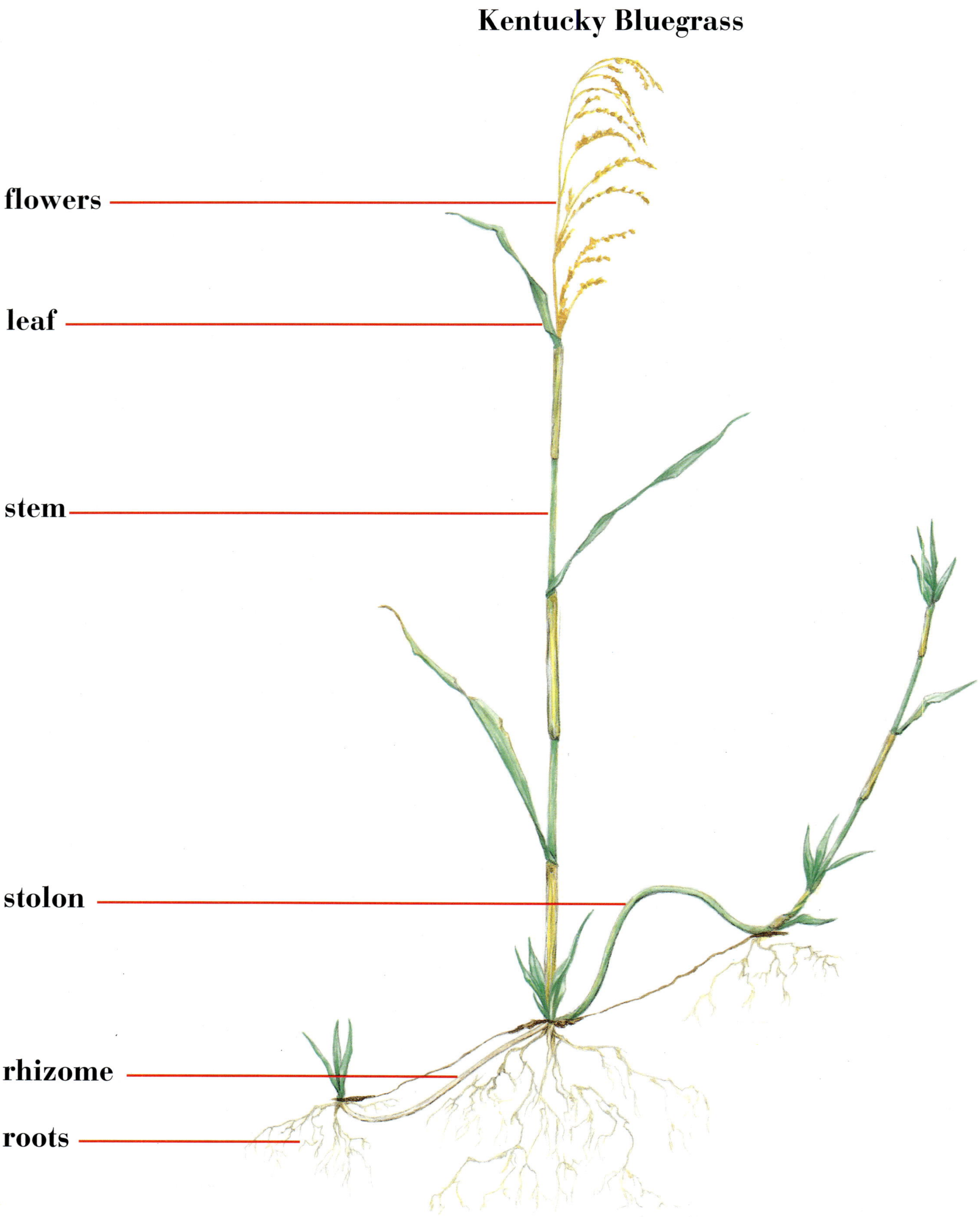

People and animals eat grasses.

There are many kinds of grass.

Oats

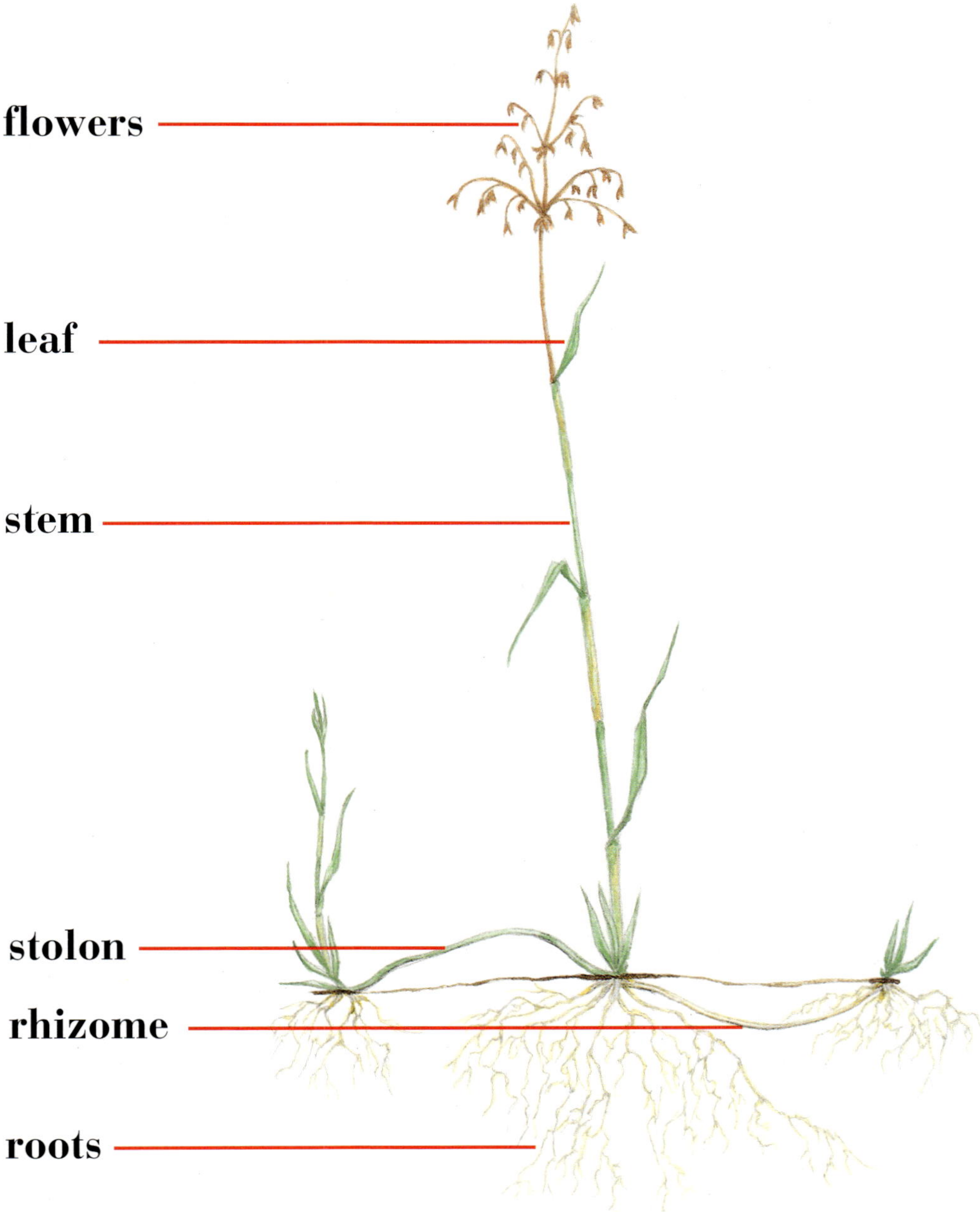

Prairie

ground squirrel | bison | prairie dog | buffalo grass

TUNNEL TOWN

Prairie dogs live in a group of underground tunnels called a town. They have food rooms, baby rooms and bathrooms!

The North American prairie early in the morning.

Savanna

red oat grass
Thomson's gazelle
termite
rhinoceros
ostrich
cheetah
secretary bird

An African savanna during the day.

SNACK ON A BACK

Oxpecker birds help other animals by eating the ticks that live on their skin and bite them.

Tundra

CHANGING COLORS

Being white makes it easier to hide in snow. Animals such as the ermine, ptarmigan and arctic fox grow darker coats for summer camouflage.

The Arctic tundra early in winter.

Air Up Close

Air is made up of invisible gases that people, animals and plants breathe. What else is in air?

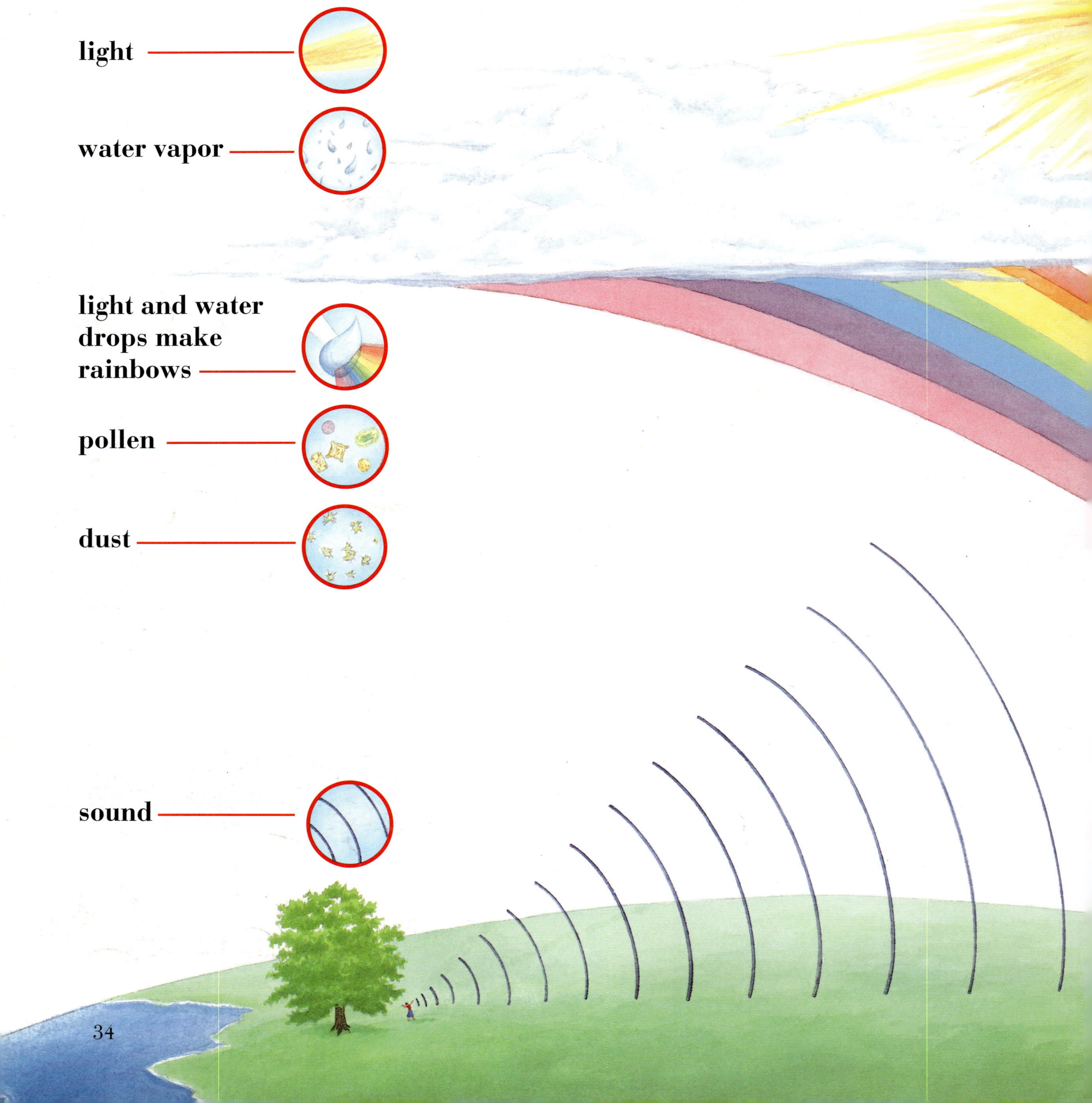

People, animals and plants need air to breathe.

Air can move quickly or slowly.

breeze

wind

gale

tornado

hurricane

Desert

desert cape hare
agama
sidewinder viper
calligonum
sedge
scorpion
hoopoe lark
oryx

The Arabian Desert in the morning.

SEA OF SAND

The wind shapes sand into hills called dunes. Sand dunes are always being moved around, and when the wind gets really strong, it makes sand storms.

Water Up Close

What is in water?

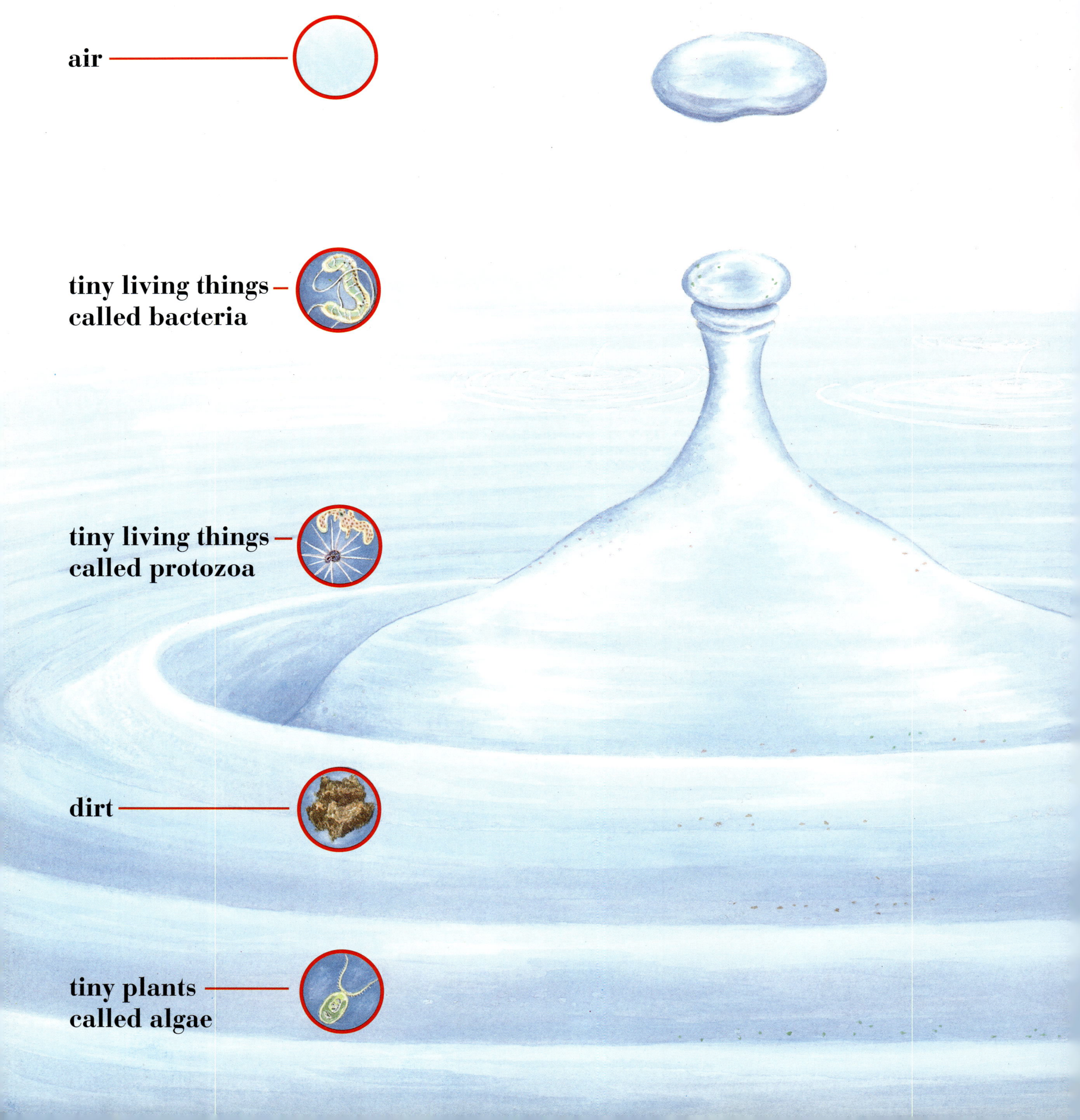

People, animals and plants need water to drink.

Water comes in different forms.

clouds

rain

fog

hail

snow

Lake

fishing spider
whirligig beetle
moorhen
duckweed
dragonfly
frog
harvest mouse
newt

A small western European lake in the morning.

A LAKE IN WINTER

Only the top of the lake freezes. Animals such as fish and frogs live under the ice during the winter.

River

harlequin duck — rainbow trout — river otter — dipper

WHERE RIVERS BEGIN

A river can begin as a small trickle of water. It flows until it meets a creek and makes it bigger. Then that creek makes another creek bigger, and so on, until the moving water becomes a river.

A North American river in the afternoon.

Ocean

The middle of the Atlantic Ocean.

MAKING CLOUDS

When the wind blows across the ocean, it picks up many tiny drops of water. As the wind collects more and more drops, they push together and make clouds.

Coral Reef

sea star
potato cod
moray eel
parrotfish
clownfish
octopus
damselfish
butterflyfish

Australia's Great Barrier Reef during the day.

CORAL AT NIGHT

Corals poke out of their hard skeletons to catch food. They wave their tentacles to find tiny floating creatures to eat.

More About ...

Algae: A group of water plants that can be as small as microscopic single cells or as large as giant kelp. Every cell on each plant's surface can absorb the nutrients it needs.

Amphibians: A group of animals that are cold-blooded and depend on the environment to heat and cool their bodies. Most amphibians are born and grow up in the water and live as adults on land near water.

Arachnids: A group of animals that have eight walking legs, but no antennae, wings or compound eyes. Every arachnid has a pair of fang-like mouthparts in front of its mouth opening, and behind this it has a pair of leg- or pincer-like appendages.

Bacteria: Microscopic single-celled life forms that grow on and inside all living things, soils and water. They may be shaped like rods, spheres or spirals.

Bryophytes: A group of plants that need constant moisture. They are small and often grow along the ground in damp areas. They don't have true roots, stems or leaves.

Caecilians: A type of amphibian. Caecilians have no arms or legs, and their eyes, which are used to sense light, are covered by skin.

Camouflage: Features of an animal's appearance that make it hard to see in its natural environment. Camouflage helps some animals hide from their enemies and helps others stay hidden as they hunt for their prey.

Chrysalis: The hard case inside which a butterfly caterpillar (called a pupa at this stage) goes through a change of form called metamorphosis. It emerges from the chrysalis as a butterfly.

Coral: A type of animal with a tube-like body and a mouth opening surrounded by tentacles. Some corals have internal skeletons and some external. Most grow in large groups with their bodies joined together to form a colony.

Crustaceans: A group of mostly aquatic animals whose bodies are covered with a hard, segmented, outer skeleton called an exoskeleton. This must be shed through molting in order for the animal to grow.

Fungi: A group of plants that are parasitic or feed off dead material. Because of their structure and because they don't make food from sunlight, they are not considered true plants.

Larva: The first stage of many invertebrates (animals without backbones) such as insects, crustaceans and mollusks. It is the name used for the animal from the time it is born, or hatched, until it is ready to change into its adult form.

Lichens: A group of plants in which each individual plant is an alga and a fungus living together. Lichens usually grow on rocks and trees. The alga provides sugars for the fungus and the fungus provides water and minerals and gives the lichen its shape.

Mammals: A group of animals that maintain their own body temperature and breathe air with their lungs. Mammals give birth to live babies that are fed milk from the mother's mammary glands.

Mollusks: A group of legless animals that have soft bodies that in many cases are protected by a hard shell. Many have a "toothed tongue," called a radula, and a fold of skin that forms a pocket to protect their soft parts.

Plankton: Tiny plants (phytoplankton) and animals (zooplankton) found in oceans, lakes and other bodies of water. Phytoplankton float near the surface and use sunlight to make food. Zooplankton include larval forms of crustaceans, mollusks and other water animals.

Pollen: Produced by seed-bearing plants, pollen looks like tiny grains of dust. It contains the plant's male sex cells. Flowers must come in contact with pollen from other flowers of the same kind in order to produce fruit and therefore new seeds.

Protozoa: Single-celled life forms that are usually found in water or in some other liquids. Some drift, some crawl and some swim. They are neither plants nor animals.

Reptiles: A group of animals whose bodies are covered with dry scales. Reptiles depend on the environment to heat and cool their bodies. Most lay shelled eggs on land, but some give birth to live babies.

Rhizomes: Thick underground stems that usually grow horizontally. New plants can develop at intervals along the length of the rhizome.

Spores: Tiny reproductive cells produced by non-seed-bearing plants. Each spore can develop into a new plant.

Springtails: Small animals closely related to insects, but not true insects. Springtails live in sheltered, damp places and on the surface of water. Each springtail has a forked tail that can spring downward to send the animal up into the air.

Stolons: Slender horizontal stems, sometimes called runners, that grow along the surface of the ground. New plants can develop at intervals along the length of the stolon.

Tundra: A northern environment that contains many bogs and small lakes. There are no trees, only small shrubs, grasses, sedges, lichens and other similar plants. The tundra is completely frozen for most of the year.